OSCAR WILDE

THREE TALES

(The Selfish Giant — The Happy Prince —
The Nightingale and the Rose)

Bearbeitet von

G. M. Griffiths

Amsterdam

FERDINAND SCHÖNINGH · PADERBORN

München · Wien · Zürich
Printed in Germany
Herstellung: Ferdinand Schöningh, Paderborn
ISBN 3-506-43101-3

EINLEITUNG

Von allem, was der sehr vielseitige Schriftsteller Oscar Wilde geschrieben hat, genießen seine kurzen Erzählungen unter jugendlichen Lesern die größte Popularität. Hinter ihrer Schlichtheit verbirgt sich eine Welt von Weisheit und Poesie.

1854 in Dublin als Sohn eines berühmten Chirurgen geboren, studierte Wilde, nachdem er die Schule in seiner Heimatstadt absolviert hatte, in Oxford. Seine ersten schriftstellerischen Versuche wurden in Zeitschriften veröffentlicht und erweckten bald das Interesse der literarischen Welt. Als Dramatiker errang er später mit *Lady Windermere's Fan* und mit *An Ideal Husband* Weltruf, der mit der köstlichen Komödie *The Importance of Being Earnest* seinen Höhepunkt erreichte. Er war ein Meister des Dialogs und liebte es, seine tieferen Gefühle, seine Philosophie in der Form von Paradoxen zum Ausdruck zu bringen.

In *The House of Pomegranates*, einer Sammlung von kurzen Erzählungen, sind besonders *The Young King* und *The Fisherman and his Soul* erfüllt von tiefer Religiosität. Im Gegensatz zu diesen sprudeln *Lord Arthur Savile's Crime*, *The Canterville Ghost* etc. geradezu über von Humor.

Sein größtes Prosawerk, *The Picture of Dorian Gray*, darf wohl mehr oder weniger als seine eigene Lebensgeschichte angesehen werden.

Die Gedichte, namentlich *De Profundis* und *The Ballad of Reading Gaol*, sind erfüllt von tiefstem Ernst. Am vorbehaltlosesten anerkannt sind seine Prosamärchen, denen die hier vorliegenden Erzählungen entnommen sind. Sie bringen ein zart soziales Gefühl zum Ausdruck, sind in prunkvoller Prosa geschrieben und von keltischer Phantasie beseelt.

Man darf wohl ohne Bedenken Oscar Wilde als einen der vielseitigsten Schriftsteller bezeichnen, die Großbritannien in der neueren Zeit hervorgebracht hat. Er starb 1900 in Paris.

THE SELFISH GIANT

Every afternoon, as they were coming from school, the children used to go and play in the Giant's garden.

It was a large lovely garden, with soft green grass. Here and there over the grass stood beautiful flowers like stars, and there were twelve peach-trees that in the springtime broke out into delicate blossoms of pink and pearl, and in the autumn bore rich fruit. The birds sat on the trees and sang so sweetly that the children used to stop their games in order to listen to them. "How happy we are here!" they cried to each other.

One day the Giant came back. He had been to visit his friend the Cornish ogre, and had stayed with him for seven years. After the seven years were over, he had said all that he had to say, for his conversation was limited, and he determined to return to his own castle. When he arrived, he saw the children playing in the garden.

"What are you doing here?" he cried in a very gruff voice, and the children ran away.

"My own garden is my own garden," said the Giant, "anyone can understand that, and I will allow nobody to play in it but myself." So he built a high wall all round it, and put up a notice-board:

TRESPASSERS will be PROSECUTED

He was a very selfish Giant.

The poor children had now nowhere to play. They tried to play on the road, but the road was very dusty and full of hard stones, and they did not like it. They used to wander round the high wall when their lessons were over, and talk about the beautiful garden inside. "How happy we were there," they said to each other.

Then the Spring came, and all over the country there were little blossoms and little birds. Only in the garden of the Selfish Giant it was still Winter. The birds did not care to sing in it as there were no children there, and the trees forgot to blossom. Once a beautiful flower put its head out from the grass, but when it saw the notice-board, it was so sorry for the children that it slipped back into the ground again and went off to sleep. The only people who were pleased were the Snow and the Frost. "Spring has forgotten this garden," they cried, "so we will live here all the year round." The Snow covered up the grass with her great white cloak, and the Frost painted all the trees silver. Then they invited the North Wind to stay with them, and he came. He was wrapped in furs, and he roared about the garden, and blew the chimney-pots down. "This is a delightful spot," he said, "we must ask the Hail on a visit." So the Hail came. Every day for three hours he rattled on the roof of the castle till he broke most of the slates, and then he ran round and round the garden as fast as he could go. He was dressed in grey, and his breath was like ice.

"I cannot understand why the Spring is so late in coming," said the Selfish Giant as he sat at the window and looked out at his cold, white garden; "I hope there will be a change in the weather."

But the Spring never came, nor the Summer. The Autumn gave golden fruit to every garden, but to the Giant's garden she gave none. "He is too selfish," she said. So it was always Winter there, and the North

Wind, and the Hail, and the Frost, and the Snow danced about through the trees.

One morning the Giant was lying awake in bed when he heard some lovely music. It sounded so sweet to his ears that he thought it must be the King's musicians passing by. It was really only a little linnet singing outside his window, but it was so long since he had heard a bird sing in his garden that it seemed to him to be the most beautiful music in the world. Then the Hail stopped dancing over his head, and the North Wind ceased roaring, and a delicious perfume came to him through the open casement. "I believe the Spring has come at last," said the Giant, and he jumped out of bed and looked out.

What did he see?

He saw a most wonderful sight. Through a little hole in the wall the children had crept in, and they were sitting in the branches of the trees. In every tree that he could see there was a little child. And the trees were so glad to have the children back again that they had covered themselves with blossoms, and were waving their arms gently above the children's heads. The birds were flying about and twittering with delight, and the flowers were looking up through the grass and laughing. It was a lovely scene, only in one corner it was still Winter. It was the farthest corner of the garden, and in it was standing a little boy. He was so small that he could not reach up to the branches of the tree, and he was wandering all round it, crying bitterly. The poor tree was still quite covered with frost and snow, and the North Wind was blowing and roaring above it. "Climb up, little boy," said the tree, and it bent its branches down as low as it could; but the boy was too tiny.

And the Giant's heart melted as he looked out. "How selfish I have been," he said, "now I know why the Spring would not come here. I will put the poor little boy on the top of the tree, and then I will knock down the wall, and my garden shall be the children's playground for ever and ever." He was really very sorry for what he had done.

So he crept downstairs and opened the front-door quite softly, and went out into the garden. But when the children saw him, they were so frightened that they all ran away, and the garden became Winter again. Only the little boy did not run, for his eyes were so full of tears that he did not see the Giant coming. And the Giant stole up behind him and took him gently in his hand and put him up into the tree. And the tree broke at once into blossom, and the birds came and sang on it, and the little boy stretched out his two arms and flung them round the Giant's neck and kissed him. And the other children, when they saw that the Giant was not wicked any longer, came running back, and with them came the Spring. "It is your garden now, little children," said the Giant, and he took a great axe and knocked down the wall. And when the people were going to market at twelve o'clock, they found the Giant playing with the children in the most beautiful garden they had ever seen.

All day long they played, and in the evening they came to the Giant to bid him good-bye.

"But where is your little companion?" he said, "the boy I put into the tree?" The Giant loved him the best because he had kissed him.

"We don't know," answered the children, "he has gone away."

"You must tell him to be sure to come here to-morrow," said the Giant. But the children said they did not know where he lived, and had never seen him before; and the Giant felt very sad.

Every afternoon, when school was over, the children came and played with the Giant. But the little boy whom the Giant loved was never seen again. The Giant was very kind to all the children, yet he longed for his first little friend and often spoke of him. "How I would like to see him!" he used to say.

Years went over, and the Giant grew very old and feeble. He could not play about any more, so he sat in a huge armchair, and watched the children at their games, and admired his garden. "I have many beautiful flowers," he said, "but the children are the most beautiful flowers of all."

One winter morning he looked out of his window as he was dressing. He did not hate the Winter now, for he knew that it was merely the Spring asleep, and that the flowers were resting.

Suddenly he rubbed his eyes in wonder, and looked and looked. It certainly was a marvellous sight. In the farthest corner of the garden was a tree quite covered with lovely blossoms. Its branches were all golden, and silver fruit hung down from them, and underneath it stood the little boy he had loved.

Downstairs ran the Giant in great joy, and out into the garden. He hastened across the grass and came near to the child. And when he came quite close, his face grew red with anger, and he said: "Who hath dared to wound thee?" For on the palms of the child's hands were the prints of two nails, and the prints of two nails were on the little feet.

"Who hath dared to wound thee?" cried the Giant. "Tell me that I may take my big sword and slay him."

"Nay!" answered the child, "but these are the wounds of Love."

"Who art thou?" said the Giant, and a strange awe fell on him, and he knelt before the little child.

And the child smiled on the Giant, and said to him: "You let me play once in your garden, to-day you shall come with me to my garden, which is Paradise."

And when the children ran in that afternoon, they found the Giant lying dead under the tree, all covered with white blossoms.

THE HAPPY PRINCE

High above the city, on a tall column, stood the statue of the Happy Prince. He was gilded all over with thin leaves of fine gold, for eyes he had two bright sapphires, and a large red ruby glowed on his sword-hilt.

He was very much admired indeed. "He is as beautiful as a weathercock," remarked one of the Town Councillors who wished to gain a reputation for having artistic tastes; "only not quite so useful," he added, fearing that people might think him unpractical, which he really was not.

"Why can't you be like the Happy Prince?" asked a sensible mother of her little boy who was crying for the moon. "The Happy Prince never dreams of crying for anything." "I am glad that there is some one in the world who is quite happy," muttered a disappointed man as he gazed at the wonderful statue.

"He looks just like an angel," said the Charity Children as they came out of the cathedral in their bright scarlet cloaks and their clean white pinafores.

"How do you know?" said the Mathematical Master. "You have never seen one."

"Ah! but we have, in our dreams," answered the children; and the Mathematical Master frowned and looked very severe, for he did not approve of children dreaming.

One night there flew over the city a little Swallow. His friends had gone away to Egypt six weeks before, but he had stayed behind, for he was in love with the most beautiful Reed. He had met her early in spring as he was flying down the river after a big yellow moth, and had been so attracted by her slender waist that he had stopped to talk to her.

"Shall I love you?" said the Swallow, who liked to come to the point at once, and the Reed made him a low bow. So he flew round and round her, touching the water with his wings, and making silver ripples. This was his courtship, and it lasted all through the summer.

"It is a ridiculous attachment," twittered the other swallows, "she has no money, and far too many relations;" and indeed the river was quite full of Reeds. Then, when the autumn came, they all flew away.

After they had gone, he felt lonely, and he began to tire of his lady-love. "She has no conversation," he said, "and I am afraid that she is a coquette, for she is always flirting with the wind." And certainly, whenever the wind blew, the Reed made the most graceful curtseys. "I admit that she is domestic," he continued, "but I love travelling, and my wife consequently should love travelling also."

"Will you come away with me?" he said finally to her; but the Reed shook her head, she was so attached to her home.

"You have been trifling with me," he cried. "I am off to the Pyramids. Good-bye!" and he flew away.

All day long he flew, and at night-time he arrived at the city. "Where shall I put up?" he said. "I hope the town has made preparations."

Then he saw the statue on the tall column.

"I will put up there," he cried. "It is a fine position with plenty of fresh air." So he alighted just between the feet of the Happy Prince.

"I have a golden bedroom," he said softly to himself as he looked round, and he prepared to go to sleep; but just as he was putting his head under his wing, a large drop of water fell on him.

"What a curious thing!" he cried. "There is not a single cloud in the sky, the stars are quite clear and bright, and yet it is raining. The climate in the north of Europe is really dreadful. The Reed used to like the rain, but that was merely her selfishness."

Then another drop fell.

"What is the use of a statue if it cannot keep the rain off?" he said. "I must look for a good chimney-pot," and he determined to fly away.

But before he had opened his wings, a third drop fell, and he looked up, and saw —— Ah! what did he see?

The eyes of the Happy Prince were filled with tears, and tears were running down his golden cheeks. His face was so beautiful in the moonlight that the little Swallow was filled with pity.

"Who are you?" he said.

"I am the Happy Prince."

"Why are you weeping then?" asked the Swallow. "You have quite drenched me."

"When I was alive and had a human heart," answered the statue, "I did not know what tears were, for I lived in the Palace of Sans-Souci, where sorrow is not allowed to enter. In the daytime I played with my companions in the garden, and in the evening I led the dance in the Great Hall. Round the garden ran a very lofty wall, but I never cared to ask what lay beyond it, everything about me was so beautiful. My courtiers called me the Happy Prince, and happy indeed I was, if pleasure is happiness. So I lived, and so I died. And now that I am dead, they have set me up here so high that I can see all the ugliness and all the misery of my city, and though my heart is made of lead, yet I cannot choose but weep."

"What! Is he not solid gold?" said the Swallow to himself. He was too polite to make any personal remark out loud.

"Far away," continued the statue in a low musical voice, "far away in a little street there is a poor house. One of the windows is open, and through it I can see a woman seated at a table. Her face is thin and worn, and she has coarse, red hands, all pricked by the needle, for she is a seamstress. She is embroidering passion-flowers on a satin gown for the loveliest of the Queen's maids-of-honour to wear at the next court-ball. In a bed in the corner of the room her little boy is lying ill. He has a fever, and is asking for oranges. His mother has nothing to give him but river water, so he is crying. Swallow, Swallow, little Swallow, will you not take her the ruby out of my sword-hilt? My feet are fastened to this pedestal and I cannot move."

"I am waited for in Egypt," said the Swallow. "My friends are flying up and down the Nile, and are talking to the large lotus-flowers. Soon they will go to sleep in the tomb of the great King. The King is there himself in his painted coffin. He is wrapped in yellow linen and embalmed with spices. Round his neck is a chain of pale green jade, and his hands are like withered leaves."

"Swallow, Swallow, little Swallow," said the Prince, "will you not stay with me one night and be my messenger? The boy is so thirsty and the mother so sad."

"I don't think I like boys," answered the Swallow. "Last summer, when I was staying on the river, there were two rude boys, the miller's sons, who were always throwing stones at me. They never hit me, of course, we swallows fly far too well for that, and besides, I come of a family famous for its agility; but still, it was a mark of disrespect."

But the Happy Prince looked so sad that the little Swallow was sorry. "It is cold here," he said, "but I will stay with you for one night, and be your messenger."

"Thank you, little Swallow," said the Prince.

So the Swallow picked out the great ruby from the Prince's sword and flew away with it in his beak over the roofs of the town.

He passed by the cathedral tower, where the white marble angels were sculptured. He passed by the palace and heard the sound of dancing. A beautiful girl came out on the balcony with her lover. "How wonderful the stars are," he said to her, "and how wonderful is the power of love!"

"I hope my dress will be ready in time for the State-ball," she answered; "I have ordered passion-flowers to be embroidered on it, but the seamstresses are so lazy."

He passed over the river and saw the lanterns hanging to the masts of the ships. He passed over the Ghetto, and saw the old Jews bargaining with each other, and weighing out money in copper scales. At last he came to the poor house and looked in. The boy was tossing feverishly on his bed, and the mother had fallen asleep, she was so tired. In he hopped, and laid the great ruby on the table beside the woman's thimble. Then he flew gently round the bed, fanning the boy's forehead with his wings. "How cool I feel," said the boy, "I must be getting better," and he sank into a delicious slumber.

Then the Swallow flew back to the Happy Prince and told him what he had done. "It is curious," he remarked, "but I feel quite warm now, although it is so cold."

"That is because you have done a good action," said the Prince. And the little Swallow began to think, and then he fell asleep. Thinking always made him sleepy.

When day broke, he flew down to the river and had a bath. "What a remarkable phenomenon," said the Professor of Ornithology as he was passing over the bridge. "A swallow in winter!" And he wrote a long letter about it to the local newspaper. Every one quoted it, it was full of so many words that they could not understand.

"To-night I go to Egypt," said the Swallow, and he was in high spirits at the prospect. He visited all the public monuments, and sat a long time on top of the church steeple. Wherever he went, the Sparrows chirruped and said to each other, "What a distinguished stranger!" So he enjoyed himself very much.

When the moon rose, he flew back to the Happy Prince.

"Have you any commissions for Egypt?" he cried, "I am just starting."

"Swallow, Swallow, little Swallow," said the Prince, "will you not stay with me one night longer?"

"I am waited for in Egypt," answered the Swallow. "To-morrow my friends will fly up to the Second Cataract. The river-horse couches there among the bulrushes, and on a great granite throne sits the God Memnon. All night long he watches the stars, and when the morning-star shines, he utters one cry of joy, and then he is silent. At noon the yellow lions come down to the water's edge to drink. They have eyes like green beryls, and their roar is louder than the roar of the cataract."

"Swallow, Swallow, little Swallow," said the Prince, "far away across the city I see a young man in a garret. He is leaning over a desk covered with papers, and in a tumbler by his side there is a bunch of withered violets. His hair is brown and crisp, and his lips are red as pomegranates, and he has large and dreamy eyes. He is trying to finish a play for the Director of the Theatre, but he is too cold to write any more. There is no fire in the grate, and hunger has made him faint."

"I will wait with you one night longer," said the Swallow, who really had a kind heart. "Shall I take him another ruby?"

"Alas! I have no ruby now," said the Prince, "my eyes are all that I have left. They are made of rare sapphires which were brought out of India a thousand years ago. Pluck out one of them and take it to him. He will sell it to the jeweller, and will buy firewood, and finish his play."

"Dear Prince," said the Swallow, "I cannot do that," and he began to weep.

"Swallow, Swallow, little Swallow," said the Prince, "do as I command you."

So the Swallow plucked out the Prince's eye, and flew away to the student's garret. It was easy enough to get in, as there was a hole in the roof. Through this he darted, and came into the room. The young man had his head buried in his hands, so he did not hear the flutter of the bird's wings, and when he looked up,he found the beautiful sapphire lying on the withered violets.

"I am beginning to be appreciated," he cried. "This is from some great admirer. Now I can finish my play," and he looked quite happy.

The next day the Swallow flew down to the harbour. He sat on the mast of a large vessel and watched the sailors hauling big chests out of the hold with ropes. "Heave a-hoy!" they shouted to each other as each chest came up. "I am going to Egypt," cried the Swallow, but nobody minded, and when the moon rose, he flew back to the Happy Prince.

"I am come to bid you good-bye," he cried. "Swallow, Swallow, little Swallow," said the Prince, "will you not stay with me one night longer?"

"It is winter," answered the Swallow, "and the chill snow will soon be here. In Egypt the sun is warm on the green palm-trees, and the crocodiles lie in the mud and look lazily about them. My companions are building a nest in the Temple of Baalbeck, and the pink and white doves are watching them and cooing to each other. Dear Prince, I must leave you, but I will never forget you, and next spring I will bring you back two beautiful jewels in place of those you have given away. The ruby shall be redder than a red rose, and the sapphire shall be as blue as the great sea."

"In the square below," said the Happy Prince, "there stands a little match-girl. She has let her matches fall in the gutter and they are all spoiled. Her father will beat her if she does not bring home some money, and she is crying. She has no shoes and stockings, and her little head is bare. Pluck out my other eye and give it to her, and her father will not beat her."

"I will stay with you one night longer," said the Swallow, but I cannot pluck out your eye. You would be quite blind then."

"Swallow, Swallow, little Swallow", said the Prince, "do as I command you."

So he plucked out the Prince's other eye, and darted down with it. He swooped past the match-girl, and slipped the jewel into the palm of her hand. "What a lovely bit of glass," cried the little girl, and she ran home, laughing.

Then the Swallow came back to the Prince. "You are blind now," he said, "so I will stay with you always."

"No, little Swallow," said the poor Prince, "you must go away to Egypt."

"I will stay with you always," said the Swallow, and he slept at the Prince's feet.

All the next day he sat on the Prince's shoulder, and told him stories of what he had seen in strange lands. He told him of the red ibises, who stand in long rows on the banks of the Nile and catch gold-fish in their beaks; of the Sphinx, who is as old as the world itself, and lives in the desert, and knows everything; of the merchants, who walk slowly by the side of their camels, and carry amber beads in their hands; of the King of the Mountains of the Moon, who is as black as ebony and worships a large crystal; of the great green snake that sleeps in a palm-tree and has twenty priests to feed it with honey-cakes; and of the pygmies who sail over the big lake on large flat leaves, and are always at war with the butterflies.

"Dear little Swallow," said the Prince, "you tell me of marvellous things, but more marvellous than anything is the suffering of men and of women. There is no Mystery so great as Misery. Fly over my city, little Swallow, and tell me what you see there."

So the Swallow flew over the great city, and saw the rich making merry in their beautiful houses, while the beggars were sitting at the gates. He flew into dark lanes and saw the white faces of starving children looking out listlessly at the black streets. Under the archway of a bridge two little boys were lying in one another's arms to try to keep themselves warm. "How hungry we are!" they said. "You must not lie here," shouted the Watchman, and they wandered out into the rain.

Then he flew back and told the Prince what he had seen.

"I am covered with fine gold," said the Prince, "you must take it off, leaf by leaf, and give it to my poor; the living always think that gold can make them happy."

Leaf after leaf of the fine gold the Swallow picked off, till the Happy Prince looked quite dull and grey. Leaf after leaf of the fine gold he brought to the poor, and the children's faces grew rosier, and they laughed and played games in the street. "We have bread now!" they cried.

Then the snow came, and after the snow came the frost. The streets looked as if they were made of silver, they were so bright and glistening; long icicles like crystal daggers hung down from the eaves of the houses, everybody went about in furs, and the little boys wore scarlet caps and skated on the ice.

The poor little Swallow grew colder and colder, but he would not leave the Prince, he loved him too well. He picked up crumbs outside the baker's door when the baker was not looking, and tried to keep himself warm by flapping his wings.

But at last he knew that he was going to die. He had just strength to fly up to the Prince's shoulder once more. "Good-bye, dear Prince," he murmured, "will you let me kiss your hand?"

"I am glad that you are going to Egypt at last, little Swallow," said the Prince, "you have stayed too long here; but you must kiss me on the lips, for I love you."

"It is not to Egypt that I am going," said the Swallow. "I am going to the House of Death. Death is the brother of Sleep, is he not?"

And he kissed the Happy Prince on the lips, and fell down dead at his feet.

At that moment a curious crack sounded inside the statue, as if something had broken. The fact is that the leaden heart had snapped right in two. It certainly was a dreadfully hard frost.

Early the next morning the Mayor was walking in the square below in company with the Town Councillors. As they passed the column, he looked up at the statue. "Dear me! How shabby the Happy Prince looks!" he said.

"How shabby indeed!" cried the Town Councillors, who always agreed with the Mayor; and they went up to look at it.

"The ruby has fallen out of his sword, his eyes are gone, and he is golden no longer," said the Mayor. "In fact he is little better than a beggar!"

"Little better than a beggar," said the Town Councillors.

"And here is actually a dead bird at his feet!" continued the Mayor. "We must really issue a proclamation that birds are not to be allowed to die here." And the Town Clerk made a note of the suggestion.

So they pulled down the statue of the Happy Prince.

"As he is no longer beautiful, he is no longer useful," said the Art Professor at the University.

Then they melted the statue in a furnace, and the Mayor held a meeting of the Corporation to decide what was to be done with the metal. "We must have another statue, of course," he said, "and it shall be a statue of myself."

"Of myself," said each of the Town Councillors, and they quarrelled. When I last heard of them, they were quarrelling still.

"What a strange thing!" said the overseer of the workmen at the foundry. "This broken heart will not melt in the furnace. We must throw it away." So they threw it on a dust-heap where the dead Swallow was also lying.

"Bring me the two most precious things in the city," said God to one of His Angels; and the Angel brought Him the leaden heart and the dead bird.

"You have rightly chosen," said God, "for in my Garden of Paradise this little bird shall sing for evermore, and in my city of gold the Happy Prince shall praise me."

"She said that she would dance with me if I brought her red roses," cried the young Student, "but in all my garden there is no red rose."

From her nest in the holm-oak tree the Nightingale heard him, and she looked out through the leaves and wondered.

"No red rose in all my garden!" he cried, and his beautiful eyes filled with tears. "Ah, on what little things does happiness depend! I have read all that the wise men have written, and all the secrets of philosophy are mine, yet for want of a red rose is my life made wretched."

"Here at last is a true lover," said the Nightingale. "Night after night have I sung of him, though I knew him not; night after night have I told his story to the stars, and now I see him. His hair is dark as the hyacinth-blossom, and his lips are red as the rose of his desire; but passion has made his face like pale ivory, and sorrow has set her seal upon his brow."

"The Prince gives a ball to-morrow night," murmured the young Student, "and my love will be of the company. If I bring her a red rose, she will dance with me till dawn. If I bring her a red rose, I shall hold her in my arms, and she will lean her head upon my shoulder, and her hand will be clasped in mine. But there is no red rose in my garden, so I shall sit lonely, and she will pass me by. She will have no heed of me, and my heart will break."

"Here indeed is the true lover," said the Nightingale. "What I sing of, he suffers, what is joy to me, to him is pain. Surely love is a wonderful thing. It is more precious than emeralds, and dearer than fine opals.

Pearls and pomegranates cannot buy it, nor is it set forth in the market-place. It may not be purchased of the merchants, nor can it be weighed out in the balance for gold."

"The musicians will sit in their gallery," said the young Student, "and play upon their stringed instruments, and my love will dance to the sound of the harp and the violin. She will dance so lightly that her feet will not touch the floor, and the courtiers in their gay dresses will throng round her. But with me she will not dance, for I have no red rose to give her," and he flung himself down on the grass, and buried his face in his hands, and wept.

"Why is he weeping?" asked a little Green Lizard, as he ran past him with his tail in the air.

"Why, indeed?" said a Butterfly, who was fluttering about after a sunbeam.

"Why, indeed?" whispered a Daisy to his neighbour, in a soft, low voice.

"He is weeping for a red rose," said the Nightingale.

"For a red rose!" they cried. "How very ridiculous!" and the little Lizard, who was something of a cynic, laughed outright.

But the Nightingale understood the secret of the Student's sorrow, and she sat silent in the oak-tree, and thought about the mystery of Love.

Suddenly she spread her brown wings for flight, and soared into the air. She passed through the grove like a shadow, and like a shadow she sailed across the garden.

In the centre of the grass-plot was standing a beautiful Rose-tree, and when she saw it, she flew over to it, and lit upon a spray.

"Give me a red rose," she cried, "and I will sing you my sweetest song."

But the Tree shook its head.

"My roses are white," it answered, "as white as the foam of the sea, and whiter than the snow upon the mountain. But go to my brother who grows round the old sun-dial, and perhaps he will give you what you want."

So the Nightingale flew over to the Rose-tree that was growing round the old sun-dial.

"Give me a red rose," she cried, "and I will sing you my sweetest song."

But the Tree shook its head.

"My roses are yellow," it answered, "as yellow as the hair of the mermaiden who sits upon an amber throne, and yellower than the daffodil that blooms in the meadow before the mower comes with his scythe. But go to my brother who grows beneath the Student's window, and perhaps he will give you what you want."

So the Nightingale flew to the Rose-tree that was growing beneath the Student's window.

"Give me a red rose," she cried, "and I will sing you my sweetest song."

But the Tree shook its head.

"My roses are red," it answered, "as red as the feet of the dove, and redder than the great fans of coral that wave in the ocean-cavern. But the winter has chilled my veins, and the frost has nipped my buds, and the storm has broken my branches, and I shall have no roses at all this year."

"One red rose is all I want," cried the Nightingale, "only one red rose! Is there no way by which I can get it?"

"There is a way," answered the Tree; "but it is so terrible that I dare not tell it to you."

"Tell it to me," said the Nightingale, "I am not afraid."

"If you want a red rose," said the Tree, "you must build it out of music by moonlight, and stain it with your own heart's blood. You must sing to me with your breast against a thorn. All night long you must sing to me, and the thorn must pierce your heart, and your life-blood must flow into my veins, and become mine."

"Death is a great price to pay for a red rose," cried the Nightingale, "and Life is very dear to all. It is pleasant to sit in the green wood, and to watch the Sun in his chariot of gold, and the Moon in her chariot of pearl. Sweet is the scent of the hawthorn, and sweet are the blue-bells that hide in the valley, and the heather that blows on the hill. Yet Love is better than Life, and what is the heart of a bird compared with the heart of a man?"

So she spread her brown wings for flight, and soared into the air. She swept over the garden like a shadow, and like a shadow she sailed through the grove.

The young Student was still lying on the grass where she had left him, and the tears were not yet dry in his beautiful eyes.

"Be happy," cried the Nightingale, "be happy; you shall have your red rose. I will build it out of music by moonlight, and stain it with my own heart's blood. All that I ask of you in return is that you will be a true lover, for Love is wiser than Philosophy, though she is wise, and mightier than Power, though he is mighty. Flame-coloured are his wings, and coloured like flame is his body. His lips are sweet as honey, and his breath is like frankincense."

The Student looked up from the grass, and listened, but he could not understand what the Nightingale was saying to him, for he only knew the things that are written down in books.

But the Oak-tree understood, and felt sad, for he was very fond of the little Nightingale who had built her nest in his branches.

"Sing me one last song," he whispered. "I shall feel very lonely when you are gone."

So the Nightingale sang to the Oak-tree, and her voice was like water bubbling from a silver jar.

When she had finished her song, the Student got up, and pulled a note-book and a lead-pencil out of his pocket.

"She has form," he said to himself, as he walked away through the grove, "that cannot be denied her, but has she got feeling? I am afraid not. In fact, she is like all artists, she is all style, without any sincerity. She would not sacrifice herself for others. She thinks merely of music, and everybody knows that the arts are selfish. Still, it must be admitted that she has some beautiful notes in her voice. What a pity it is that they do not mean anything, or do any practical good." And he went into his room, and lay down on his little pallet-bed, and began to think of his love; and after a time, he fell asleep.

And when the Moon shone in the heavens, the Nightingale flew to the Rose-tree, and set her breast against the thorn. All night long she sang with her breast against the thorn, and the cold crystal Moon leaned down and listened. All night long she sang and the thorn went deeper into her breast, and her life-blood ebbed away from her.

She sang of the birth of love in the heart of a boy and a girl. And on the topmost spray of the Rose-tree there blossomed a marvellous rose, petal following petal, as song followed song. Pale was it at first, as the mist that hangs over the river — pale as the feet of the morning, and silver as the wings of the dawn. As the shadow of a rose in a mirror of silver, as the shadow of a rose in a water-pool, so was the rose that blossomed on the topmost spray of the Tree.

But the Tree cried to the Nightingale to press closer against the thorn. "Press closer, little Nightingale," cried the Tree, "or the Day will come before the Rose is finished."

So the Nightingale pressed closer against the thorn, and louder and louder grew her song, for she sang of the Birth of passion in the soul of a man and a maid.

And a delicate flush of pink came into the leaves of the rose, like the flush in the face of the bridegroom when he kisses the lips of the bride. But the thorn had not yet reached her heart, so the rose's heart remained white, for only a Nightingale's heart's blood can crimson the heart of a rose.

And the Tree cried to the Nightingale to press closer against the thorn. "Press closer, little Nightingale," cried the Tree, "or the Day will come before the rose is finished."

So the Nightingale pressed closer against the thorn, and the thorn touched her heart, and a fierce pang of pain shot through her. Bitter, bitter was the pain, and wilder and wilder grew her song, for she sang of the

Love that is perfected by Death, of the Love that dies not in the tomb.

And the marvellous rose became crimson, like the rose of the eastern sky. Crimson was the girdle of petals, and crimson as a ruby was the heart.

But the Nightingale's voice grew fainter, and her little wings began to beat, and a film came over her eyes. Fainter and fainter grew her song, and she felt something choking her in her throat.

Then she gave one last burst of music. The white Moon heard it, and she forgot the dawn, and lingered on in the sky. The red rose heard it, and it trembled all over with ecstasy, and opened its petals to the cold morning air. Echo bore it to her purple cavern in the hills, and woke the sleeping shepherds from their dreams. It floated through the reeds of the river, and they carried it to the sea.

"Look! Look!" cried the Tree, "the rose is finished now." But the Nightingale made no answer, for she was lying dead in the grass, with the thorn in her heart.

And at noon the Student opened his window and looked out.

"Why, what a wonderful piece of luck!" he cried. "Here is a red rose! I have never seen any rose like it in my life. It is so beautiful that I am sure it has a long Latin name," and he leaned down and plucked it.

Then he put on his hat, and ran up to the Professor's house with the rose in his hand.

The daughter of theProfessor was sitting in the doorway winding blue silk on a reel, and her little dog was lying at her feet.

"You said that you would dance with me if I brought you a red rose," cried the Student. "Here is the reddest rose in all the world. You will wear it to-night next your heart, and as we dance together, it will tell you how I love you."

But the girl frowned.

"I am afraid it will not go with my dress," she answered, "and besides, the Chamberlain's nephew has sent me some real jewels, and everybody knows that jewels cost far more than flowers."

"Well, upon my word, you are very ungrateful," said the Student angrily; and he threw the rose into the street, where it fell into the gutter, and a cart-wheel went over it.

"Ungrateful!" said the girl. "I tell you what, you are very rude; and after all, who are you? Only a Student. Why, I don't believe you have even got silver buckles to your shoes as the Chamberlain's nephew has," and she got up from her chair and went into the house.

"What a silly thing Love is," said the Student as he walked away. "It is not half as useful as Logic, for it does not prove anything, and it is always telling one of things that are not going to happen, and making one believe things that are not true. In fact, it is quite unpractical, and, as in this age to be practical is everything, I shall go back to Philosophy and study Metaphysics."

So he returned to his room and pulled out a great dusty book, and began to read.

ANMERKUNGEN

THE SELFISH GIANT

4. *selfish (egoistic)* eigennützig. — *giant* Riese. — *peach* Pfirsich. — *pink* rosafarben. — *pearl* mattweiß. — *Cornish* (from Cornwall, part of England). — *ogre* Ungeheuer, Menschenfresser (Märchengestalt). — *limited* begrenzt, beschränkt. — *gruff* (rough) barsch. — *notice-board* Anschlagtafel. — *trespasser* Zuwiderhandelnder. — *to prosecute* gerichtlich belangen (etwa: das Betreten dieses Gartens ist bei Strafe verboten). — *dusty* staubig.

5. *to care to* (to like) mögen. — *it was sorry for the children* die Kinder taten ihm leid. — *to slip* (to glide) gleiten. — *cloak* (coat) Mantel. — *to wrap* hüllen. — *fur* Pelz. — *chimney-pot* Schornstein. — *to rattle* rasseln. — *slate* Dachplatte.

6. *linnet* Hänfling. — *casement* Fenster. — *hole* Loch. — *to twitter* zwitschern. — *to wave* schwenken. — *to reach* reichen. — *to blow* (blew, blown) blasen, wehen. — *to bend* (bent, bent) biegen, beugen. — *tiny* (very small) winzig.

7. *to melt* schmelzen, erweichen. — *top* Spitze, Gipfel. — *to knock down* niederreißen. — *front door* Haustür. — *soft* (softly) leise, sachte. — *to fling* (flung, flung) = *to throw* (threw, thrown) werfen. — *wicked* böse, schlecht. — *to bid good-bye* (to say farewell) sich verabschieden.

8. *to long for* sich sehnen nach. — *huge* (enormous) kolossal. — *armchair* Lehnsessel. — *merely* (only) lediglich. *underneath* unter. — *close* (near) dicht bei, nah. — *hath* (old English) has. — *to dare* wagen. — *to wound* verwunden. — *thee* (old English) you. — *palm of the hand* Handfläche. — *print* Druck, Abdruck.

9. *who art thou?* (old English) who are you? — *awe* ehrfurchtsvoller Schrecken. — *knelt* (to kneel, knelt, knelt) knien.

THE HAPPY PRINCE

9. *column* Säule. — *gilded* (covered with gold) vergoldet. — *bright* (shining) leuchtend, glänzend. — *ruby* Rubin. — *sword-hilt* Degengriff. — *Town Councillor* Stadtrat. — *to gain a reputation* sich einen Namen machen. — *sensible* (reasonable) vernünftig. — *to cry for the moon* (to desire the impossible) Unmögliches verlangen. — *he never dreams of it* es fällt ihm nicht im Traume ein. — *to mutter* (to mumble) murmeln. — *to gaze at* (to stare at) anstarren.

10. *Charity children* (charity = Barmherzigkeit) Armenhauskinder. — *pinafore* Kinderschürze. — *to frown* (to look angry) die Stirn runzeln, finster blicken. — *to approve of* billigen, gutheißen. — *reed* Ried, Schilf. — *slender* schlank. — *waist* Taille. — *moth* (small butterfly) Motte, Falter. — *to come to the point* zur Sache kommen. — *at once* (immediately) sofort. — *low* (deep) tief. — *bow* Verbeugung. — *ripple* (very small wave) kleine Welle. — *courtship* (to court = den Hof machen) Werbung. — *attachment* Zuneigung. — *to twitter* (to chirrup) zwitschern. — *to tire of something* einer Sache überdrüssig werden. — *to be attached to* (to be fond of) hängen an.

11. *to trifle with* (to play with) tändeln. — *I am off* ich ziehe los. — *to put up* (to stay) logieren. — *plenty of* (ample) reichlich. — *to alight* sich niederlassen. — *use* Zweck, Nutzen. — *selfishness* (egotism) Selbstsucht. — *chimney-pot* Schornstein. — *to determine* (to resolve) beschließen. — *cheek* Wange.

12. *to drench* (to soak) durchnässen. — *lofty* (high) hoch. — *courtier* Höfling. — *the ugliness* das Häßliche. — *I cannot choose* (I cannot help) es bleibt mir nichts übrig. — *low* (soft) leise. — *worn* (to wear, wore, worn) abgehärmt. — *coarse* grob. — *to prick* stechen, zerstechen. — *seamstress* ['semstris] Näherin. — *to embroider* sticken. — *satin* Atlas. — *gown* (dress) Gewand. — *maid-of-honour* Hofdame.

13. *pedestal* ['pedistəl) Sockel. — *to be waited for* (to be expected) erwartet werden. — *tomb* [tu:m] Grabmal. — *coffin* Sarg. — *to be wrapped in* eingehüllt sein in. — *to embalm* einbalsamieren. — *spice* Spezereien. — *jade* Jade (Halbedelstein). — *to wither* verdorren. — *to hit* (hit, hit) treffen (Ziel). — *agility* Behendigkeit. — *disrespect* Respektlosigkeit. — *beak* (bill) Schnabel. — *to sculpture* meißeln, aushauen.

14. *to bargain* (to trade) handeln. — *to weigh out* auswiegen. — *scales* (Plural) Waage. — *to toss* (to throw, threw, thrown) wälzen. — *thimble* Fingerhut. — *to fan* fächeln. — *remarkable* (strange) merkwürdig. — *ornithology* Vogelkunde. — *to quote* (to cite) zitieren. — *to be in high spirits* (to be very gay) gut aufgelegt sein. — *to chirrup* (to twitter) zwitschern. — *prospect* Aussicht. — *distinguished* vornehm.

15. *commission* Auftrag. — *river-horse* (hippopotamus) Nilpferd. — *to couch* (to lie, lay, lain) liegen. — *bulrush* (large reed) Binse, Schilf. — *beryl* Beryll (ein Mineral). — *roar* Gebrüll. — *garret* Dachkammer. — *tumbler* (drinking glass) Wasserglas. — *bunch* Strauß. — *crisp* (curly) kraus. — *pomegranate* Granatapfel. — *play* Theaterstück. — *grate* (fireplace) Kamin. — *faint* (weak) schwach. — *left* übrig. — *firewood* Brennholz.

16. *to dart* (to fly fast) schießen. — *to appreciate* (to value) schätzen. — *admirer* Verehrer. — *harbour* Hafen. — *to haul* ziehen, zerren. — *rope* (thick cord) Tau. — *hold* Schiffsraum. — *heave a-hoy!* (Seemannsruf). — *to shout* (to cry loud) schreien. — *to mind* (to take notice) beachten. — *to bid good-bye* (to say farewell) sich verabschieden. — *chill* (cold) kalt. — *mud* (morass) Schlamm. — *pink* rosafarben. — *dove* Taube. — *to coo* girren.

17. *square* öffentlicher Platz. — *match-girl* kleine Streichholzverkäuferin. — *gutter* Rinnstein. — *to spoil* verderben. — *bare* (uncovered) unbedeckt. — *to swoop* (to dart) herabschießen. — *to slip* schieben, gleiten lassen. — *the palm of the hand* die Handfläche. — *amber* Bernstein; *amber beads* Bernsteinperlen.

18. *ebony* ['ebəni] Ebenholz. — *to worship* anbeten. — *pygmy* ['pigmi] (dwarf) Zwerg. — *lake* Binnensee. — *suffering* Leid, Kummer. — *to make merry* sich vergnügen. — *gate* Tor. — *lane* Gasse. — *to starve* (to die of hunger) verhungern. — *listless* (indifferent) teilnahmlos. — *dull* (dim) trübe.

19. *to glisten* (to shine) glänzen. — *icicle* Eiszapfen. — *dagger* Dolch. — *eaves* Dachrinnen. — *to flap the wings* mit den Flügeln schlagen. — *crack* (click) Knacken. — *dear me!* herrje! — *shabby* schäbig. — *to agree* (to be of the same opinion) beistimmen.

20. *to be gone* fort sein. — *to issue* erlassen. — *Town Clerk* Stadtschreiber. — *suggestion* (proposal) Vorschlag. — *to melt* schmelzen. — *furnace* Schmelzofen. — *overseer* Aufseher. — *foundry* Gießerei. — *dust-heap* Schutthaufen. — *for evermore* ewig.

THE NIGHTINGALE AND THE ROSE

21. *holm-oak* Steineiche. — *to depend on* abhängen von. — *wretched* (miserable) elend. — *hyacinth-blossom* Hyazinthenblüte. — *ivory* Elfenbein. — *seal* Stempel. — *brow* (forehead) Stirn. — *to murmur* murmeln. — *dawn* Morgendämmerung. — *to lean* lehnen. — *to have heed of* (to take notice of) beachten. — *emerald* Smaragd.

22. *pomegranate* Granatapfel, Granate. — *to set forth* ausstellen (zum Verkauf). — *to weigh* wiegen. — *stringed instrument* Streichinstrument. — *harp* Harfe. — *floor* Fußboden. — *courtier* Höfling. — *gay* bunt, farbenfreudig. — *to throng round* sich scharen um. — *to fling* (flung, flung) (=to throw, threw, thrown) werfen. — *to bury* verbergen, verstecken, eingraben. — *lizard* Eidechse. — *to flutter* flattern. — *to whisper* flüstern. — *daisy* Gänseblume. — *cynic* Zyniker. — *to laugh outright* laut heraus lachen. — *grove* Hain. — *to soar* schweben. — *grass-plot* (lawn) Rasenfläche. — *to light* (lit, lit) *upon* sich niederlassen auf. — *spray* Sproß.

23. *foam* (froth) Schaum. — *sundial* ['sʌndaiəl] Sonnenuhr. — *mermaiden* Seejungfer. — *daffodil* Narzisse. — *to bloom* (to blossom) blühen. — *mower* Schnitter. — *scythe* Sense. — *dove*

Taube. — *fan* Fächer. — *to wave* wehen. — *cavern* Höhle. — *to chill* erstarren. — *vein* Ader. — *to nip* zerstören (durch Frost). — *bud* Knospe.

24. *to stain* färben. — *to pierce* durchbohren. — *to flow* fließen. — *chariot* Wagen. — *scent* (odour) Duft. — *hawthorn* Hagedorn. — *bluebell* Glockenblume. — *to hide* (hid, hidden) verbergen. — *to blow* (blew, blown) erblühen. — *to compare* vergleichen. — *flight* Flug. — *to sweep* (swept, swept) fegen. — *in return* dafür, zum Dank. — *flame-coloured* feuerrot.

25. *frankincense* Weihrauch. — *to bubble* sprudeln. — *jar* Krug. — *notebook* Notizbuch. — *to deny* absprechen, leugnen. — *style* Stil. — *sincerity* [sin'seriti] Aufrichtigkeit. — *to admit* zugeben. — *to do any good* von Nutzen sein. — *pallet-bed* Feldbett.

26. *to ebb away* wegfließen. — *birth* Geburt. — *topmost* alleroberste. — *petal* Blumenblatt. — *mist* Dunst, leichter Nebel. — *pool* Pfuhl. — *flush* Röte. — *to crimson* rot färben. — *fierce* heftig. — *a pang of pain* heftiger Schmerz, Stich.

27. *perfected* vollendet, gekrönt. — *eastern* östlich. — *girdle* Gürtel. — *to choke* würgen. — *throat* Kehle. — *burst* Ausbruch, Schwall. — *to linger* zögern, verweilen. — *to float* schweben. — *reed* Ried. — *message* Botschaft. — *noon* Mittag (12 Uhr). — *luck* Glück. — *to pluck* (to pick) pflücken. — *to wind* [waind] (wound, wound) wickeln. — *reel* Röllchen.

28. *to frown* die Stirn runzeln, finster blicken. — *chamberlain* Kammerherr. — *gutter* Rinnstein, Gosse. — *cartwheel* Wagenrad. — *rude* ungezogen. — *buckle* Schnalle, Agraffe. — *silly* (stupid) albern, dumm. — *to prove* beweisen. — *age* Zeitalter. — *dusty* staubig.

B C D E ———— R S T U